Mohd Afizi Mohd Shukran
Norzaini Ismail

Analysis On Wi-Fi Signal Booster

Mohd Nazri Ismail
Mohd Afizi Mohd Shukran
Norzaini Ismail

Analysis On Wi-Fi Signal Booster

LAP LAMBERT Academic Publishing

Impressum / Imprint

Bibliografische Information der Deutschen Nationalbibliothek: Die Deutsche Nationalbibliothek verzeichnet diese Publikation in der Deutschen Nationalbibliografie; detaillierte bibliografische Daten sind im Internet über http://dnb.d-nb.de abrufbar.

Bibliographic information published by the Deutsche Nationalbibliothek: The Deutsche Nationalbibliothek lists this publication in the Deutsche Nationalbibliografie; detailed bibliographic data are available in the Internet at http://dnb.d-nb.de.

Coverbild / Cover image: www.ingimage.com

Verlag / Publisher:
LAP LAMBERT Academic Publishing
ist ein Imprint der / is a trademark of
OmniScriptum GmbH & Co. KG
Heinrich-Böcking-Str. 6-8, 66121 Saarbrücken, Deutschland / Germany
Email: info@lap-publishing.com

Herstellung: siehe letzte Seite /
Printed at: see last page
ISBN: 978-3-659-49603-5

Analysis on Wi-Fi Signal Booster

Authors:

Mohd Nazri Ismail

Mohd Afizi Shukuran

Kamaruzaman Maskat

TABLE OF CONTENTS

LIST OF TABLES

Page no

LIST OF FIGURES

CHAPTER 1: INTRODUCTION

The Project of **The Wifi Signal Booster with Stir Frying Pan** is opposed by the Last Semester Student of Networking System Programme as the final year project. We prefer the idea of using wireless to make things cool. This project involved both hardware and software. The project covers the element of Networking in wifi signal Booster to the general use.

A Wifi Signal Booster with stir frying pan is one of the easiest Omni-directional antennas to make at home. Benefits not solely used for frying pan, but can also are used to strengthen the wifi signal, which is now increasingly megatrend. They do intentionally use a nickname, such as familiarity with the cyber world. Pan bolic is a parabolic antenna is made from the pan. Bolic own words taken from said parabolic. Up to be Panbolic, or parabolic antenna (parabola) that is made from the pan.

Benefit Bolic from pan to strengthen own their wifi signal. The principle works the same as other parabolic antennas. That means placing the antenna on the sensitive part of the focal point parabola (pan). So, all electromagnetic waves that the pan will be collected and received by the sensitive part of the tool. Panbolic advantage, in making a very simple and requires no connection cable and connector. No need to disassemble the casing PC installation, and does not need external power supply, because the power supply from the USB port Wifi desktop or notebook PC.

To develop and determine the best low cost wireless antenna that is build using recycle parts. Booster will eliminate this difficulty for users to share and access each other information for easier communication and exchange of information. Other than that, user may choose to purchase a low cost antenna that will either provide more or parallel

7

signal strength in enhancing the signal strength or an expensive antenna.

The comparison software for detect wifi signal, such as RF spectrum, wireshark, backtrack, netstumbler and use to another software. We can used of backtrack 3 for our project because it provides an easy way to account for the usage and location of items and inventory through functions such as time and date stamping, reservations, customized reports, and bar coded labels.

1.1   Purpose and Objectives of Project

The purpose of this project is basically on the Radio Frequencies of antennas to users. In this Wi-Fi booster with frying pan project, the researcher would like to develop and determine the best low-cost wireless antenna that is build using recycle parts. Booster will eliminate this difficulty for users to share and access each other information for easier communication and exchange of information. Other than that, user may choose to purchase a low cost antenna that will either provide more or parallel signal strength in enhancing the signal strength or an expensive antenna.

1.1.1   These are several objectives of the project to be implemented:

- To develop a simple wifi booster called "Frying Pan"
- To evaluate signal strengthen performance by using wifi booster
- To expose students handle to wireless networking.
- To expose student can connect computers anywhere at home or office without the need or wires. The computers connect to the network using radio signals, and computers can be up to 100 feet or so apart.
- Students will be exposed to the wireless networking how-tos
- To achieve better wifi reception

1.2   Problem and Solving Statement

1.2.1   Problem statement

- Provide large area coverage the loss of strength when pointing the antenna to the destination during rainy days
- Wired Equivalent Privacy or WEP, has been shown to be breakable even when correctly configured
- The placement of access point is out of the line of network

1.2.2   Solving statement

- To improve the range by location additional access points
- Position the Router or Access Point Safely
- Turn off the Network during Extended Periods of Non-Use
- Analyzing and differentiates the results of a few antenna
- Collect and gather all detail of the experiment done on each antenna
- Build a conceptual model that could give similar signal strength

1.3   Exchange of information

- Parabolic antennas are the most widely used fixed broadband narrow beam antennas.
- Very large radius parabolic antennas have been used for space communication with distant spacecraft where high gain is required. However, to achieve the maximum gain from the antennas, the parabolic surface must be a perfect parabola within a small fraction of a wavelength. As the frequency increase, the surface   must   be   perfect.

9

1.4   Significant of a Research Project

- To increase the distance of the reach of wireless LAN is required to gain external antenna higher than standard antenna.
- High Gain external antenna relative expensive price
- Many items commonly found in everyday life that can be used to make the High Gain antenna with simple and soft costs.
- Also can learn a lot of new software for hacking, and also to get the signal with ease, using only items used

1.5   Scope of Work

Scope of work in the research will be as below:

- Gantt Chart technique is employed to ensure the success of our project
- The assessment covers the wireless networking devices, wireless networks,network performances and transmit to compare of the software
- Demonstration of wireless or wifi hacking using Backtrack application either on a live cd or a live usb

1.6   Limitation of Project

- Lack of information regarding the radio frequency signal wave

The equipments are:

  1) Network analyzer

  2) Spectrum analyzer

3) Radiation meter

- Backtrack not support window Vista and window 7
- Difficulty to detect WPA using Backtrack

CHAPTER 2: LITERATURE REVIEW

2.1   History wifi

"Wifi's ultimate significance may be that it provides a glimpse of what be possible with future wireless technologies". Wifi was boosted by the growing popularity of highspeed internet connection in the home. It is the easiest way to enable several computers to share a broadband link. Spread-spectrum technology called orthogonal frequency division multiplexing (OFDM) and can achieve speeds of up to 54 megabits per seconds in the 2.4GHz band.

2.2   Basic Antenna

An antenna is a conductive element which converts electrical energy into an electromagnetic field (transmit) or convert an electromagnetic field into electrical energy (receive). The same antenna can be used with the same characteristic as transmitter or as a receiver antenna. An antenna is characterized or important antenna concepts by its center frequency, bandwidth, gain, polization, radiation pattern and input impedance.

Basically any conductor or dielectric will contribute to this phenomenon. The strength of the radiated field should have a significant effect on the properties of the antenna. On top of that, radiation can be induced from any conductors or even dielectric. The reason for this is due to the fact that the electrons in the dielectric will move back and forward at radio frequency and eventually forms an accelerated charge and radiates. An antenna is an electronic component designed to send or receive radio waves.

More simply, an antenna is an arrangement of conductors designed to radiate (transmit) an electromagnetic field in response to an applied alternating electromotive force (EMF) and the associated alternating electric current.

By adding additional conducting rods or coils (called *elements)* and varying their length, spacing and orientation, an antenna with specific desired properties can be created, such as a Dish antenna. Typically, antennas are designed to operate in a relatively narrow frequency range and higher gain antennas narrower beam width and less chance of receiving interference. The design criteria for receiving and transmitting antennas differ slightly, but generally an antenna can receive and transmit equally as well as this property is called reciprocity. Types of antennas such as isotropic antenna (idealized) is radiate power equally in all direction, dipole antennas is half wave dipole antenna and quarter wave vertical antenna and parabolic reflective antenna.

A theoretical to obtain Omni-directional gain from an isotropic antenna has a perfect 360 small and larger beam width. Antenna theory dipole is energy lobes are 'pushed in' from the top and bottom higher gain is smaller vertical beam width and larger horizontal lobe. Beam width is the angular separation of the half power points of the radiated pattern.

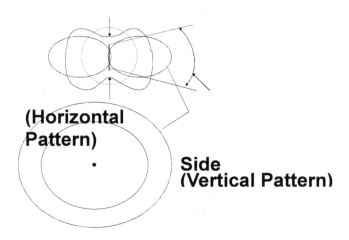

Figure 2.2.1: Vertical and Horizontal pattern view

High gain Omni-directional is more coverage area in a circular pattern. Energy level directly Figure 2.2.1 or Figure 2.2.2 the antenna will become lower.

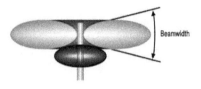

Figure 2.2.2: Pattern side

5GHz Omni-directional antennas is 28 dBi dish (H or V polarization). Figure 2.2.3

Figure 2.2.3: Omni-directional antennas Polarization side

2.2.1   Input Impedance

For an efficient transfer of energy, the impedance of the radio, of the antenna and of the transmission cable connecting must be the same. Transceivers and their transmission lines are typically designed for 50Ω impedance. If the antenna has a different from 50Ω, then there is a mismatch and an impedance matching circuit is required.

2.2.2 Directivity Gain

Directivity is the ability of an antenna to focus energy in a particular direction when transmitting, or to receive energy better from a particular direction when receiving. Gain is given in reference to a standard antenna. The two most common reference antennas are the isotropic antenna and the resonant half-wave dipole antenna. Especially antennas with high gain show side lobes in the radiation pattern side lobes are peaks in gain other than the main lobe (the "beam"). Side lobes have bad impact to the antenna quality whenever the system is being used to determine the direction of a signal, for example in RADAR systems.

2.2.3 Beamwidth

An antenna beamwidth is usually understood to mean the half-power beamwidth. The angular distance between the half power points is defined as the beamwidth. Both horizontal and vertical beamwidths are usually considered.

2.2.4 Polarization

Polarization is defined as the orientation of the electric field of an electromagnetic wave. Polarization is in general described by an ellipse. Two special cases of elliptical polarization are linear polarization and circular polarization. Omnidirectional antennas always have vertical polarization. With horizontal polarization, such reflections cause variations in received signal strength.

2.2.5 Bandwidth

The bandwidth of an antenna is defined as the range of frequencies within which the performance of an antenna conforms to a specific standard with respect to some characteristic. The bandwidth can also express as the ratio of the upper or lower frequencies of acceptable operation for wideband antenna.

2.3 Electromagnetic Waves

For this research project as well, it is intriguing to introduce the general theory of electromagnetic fields in before presenting the details about the project. Electromagnetic wave consists of a combination of oscillating electrical and magnetic fields, perpendicular to each other. This is difficult to visualize, however the waveform has similar characteristics of other types of waves. Some problems involving electric currents can be cast in equivalent forms involving magnetic currents the use of magnetic currents is simply a mathematical tool, they have never been proven to exist.

2.3.1   Electromagnetic fields are divided into four different quantities:

- The magnetic flux density B with the unit T (Telsa or volt-second per square meter)
- The magnetic field intensity H with the unit A/m (Ampere per meter)
- The electric field intensity E with the unit V/m (Volt per meter)
- The electric field flux density D with the unit C/m^2 (Coulomb per square meter)

For a time-varying electric filed (E) and flux density (D) will give rise to magnetic flux density (B) and magnetic field intensity (H). The same holds for the reverse process, however this relation depends on the properties of the medium. Under certain conditions in which the source is far considered far enough, the magnetic field intensity

16

(H) will be perpendicular to the electric field (E). Both of them will be traveling normal to direction propagation.

2.4   Basic of Parabolic and Antennas

Parabolic reflector antennas are most widely used fixed broadband wireless narrow beam antennas. They usually are configured with the feed point or driven element situated at the local point of the parabolic-shaped reflector as shown in Figure 2.4.1

If the diameter of the parabolic reflector is large compared to a wavelength, ray-tracing techniques can be used to evaluate the reflection properties of the parabola.

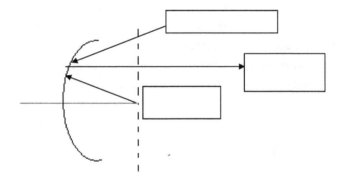

Figure 2.4.1: Parabolic reflector antennas

The parabolic reflector or dish antenna has been used far more widely in recent years with advent of satellite television (TV). However the dish antenna finds uses in many radio and wireless applications at frequencies usually above about 1GHz where very high levels of RF antenna gain are required along with narrow beamwidths.

In many professional applications these parabolic reflectors or dish antennas are used for satellite as well as for radio astronomy and it is used in many microwave links, often being seen on radio relay towers and mobile phone antenna masts. In all these applications very high levels of gain are required to receive the incoming signals that are often at a very low level. For transmitting this type of RF antenna design is able to concentrate the available radiated power into a narrow beamwidth, ensuring all the available power is radiated in the required direction.

2.4.1   Parabolic reflector basics

As we learn from the antenna RF radiation are used to illuminate a reflector is curved in the shape of a paraboloid. This form allows a highly accurate ray will be obtained. In this way, feed system of the actual transmitting antenna and parabolic reflecting surface is purely passive. Because of bolic to properly reflect the court and no interference.

When observing system of parabolic reflector antenna is a set of important parameters and terms:

- *Focus*   The focus or focal point of the parabolic reflector is the point at which any incoming signals are concentrated. When radiating from this point the signals will be reflected by the reflecting surface and travel in a parallel beam and to provide the required gain and beamwidth.
- *Vertex*   This is the innermost point at the centre of the parabolic reflector.
- *Focal length*   the focal length of a parabolic antenna is the distance from its focus to its vertex.
- *Aperture*   The aperture of a parabolic reflector is what may be termed its "opening" or the area which it covers. For a circular reflector, this is described by its diameter. It can be likened to the aperture of an optical lens.

2.4.2   Parabolic antenna focal length

One important element of a parabolic antenna is its focal length. To ensure that the antenna operates correctly, it is necessary to ensure that the radiating element is placed at the focal point. To determine this it is necessary to know the focal length.

$$\textbf{Focal length} \quad \textbf{f} = \frac{D^2}{\boxed{16\,c}}$$

Where:

  f = focal length

  D = diameter of the reflector

  c = depth of the reflector

In addition to this the f/D ratio is important. As the f/D ratio is often specified along with the diameter, the focal length can be obtained very easily by multiplying its f/D ratio by the specified diameter D.

The size of the dish is the most important factor since it determines the maximum gain that an be achieved at the given frequency and the resulting beamwidth. The ratio f/D (focal length/diameter of the dish) is the fundamental factor governing the design of the feed for a dish. The ratio is directly related to the beamwidth of the feed necessary to illuminate the dish effectively. Two dishes of the same diameter but different focal lengths require different design of feed if both are to be illuminated efficiently.

2.4.3 Feed Systems

A parabolic antenna is designed around its feed system the design of the feed system is central to the design of the overall parabolic reflector antenna system. There are two basic forms of feed system that can be used for a parabolic reflector antenna:

Focal point feed system: Using a focal point feed system the source of the radiation is placed at the focal point of the parabola and this is used to illuminate the reflector. Figure 2.4.3.1

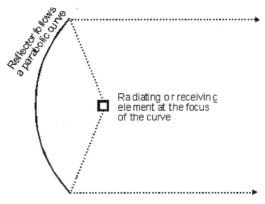

Figure 2.4.3.1: Focal point feed system

2.5 Pattern of Aperture Antennas

In optics, the term *aperture* refers to the opening through which all rays pass. For example, the aperture of a paraboloidal reflector antenna would be the plane circle, normal to the rays from a distant point source that just covers the paraboloid. The phase of the plane wave from a distant point source would be constant across the aperture plane when the aperture is perpendicular to the line-of-sight. Figure 2.5.1

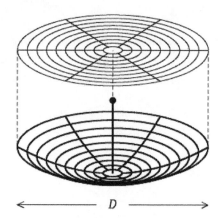

Figure 2.5.1: The aperture plane associated with a paraboloidal dish of diameter D.

2.6 Case Study: Cost-effective and painless delivery of "whole-home" wireless network coverage for integrators of wireless home automation solution.

The following is a real-world case study that exhibits the power of Luxul Wireless solutions:

Home and Network Description: A three-level 7500 square foot home using a single WAP

Located in the basement level. Due to the location of the WAP, network coverage throughout the home was spotty and incomplete on the main level and nearly non-existent on the upper level.

Test Overview Description: Signal strength and data-rate tests were conducted first with only the WAP (a popular, off the shelf router). Afterwards, the WAP was connected to the Pro-WAV 100 and the same tests were run. AirMagnet Survey (www.airmagnet.com) was used to compare the signal strengths, while IPERF (a freeware utility) was used to measure and compare data rates.

The test results reflected in this case study were performed using the following parameters:

- Test Area: 7500 sq. foot home, three floors

- Data collection tools: AirMagnet Survey and IPERF

- Access Point: Linksys WRT54G

- Access Point Power: Full Power, 18 dBm

- Baseline Antenna Configuration: Standard OEM duel dipole antennas

- Comparison Configuration: Luxul Pro-WAV 100 System connected to port 1

2.7   Case Study; On-Channel Boosters to Fill Gaps in DTV Broadcast Coverage

As of this writing, the Federal Communications Commission (FCC) has no rules in place to authorize the licensing and standard operation of DTV boosters. Translators and boosters for analog TV service are covered under part 74 along with LPTV service. Similarly as of this writing, no regulations are in place to authorize standard operation of DTV service with translators or in LPTV. This author believes that there are presently substantial areas that lie well within the defined service areas of many DTV broadcast stations yet they are essentially terrain-shielded from adequate DTV coverage. The problem is especially acute in mountainous areas.A possible fast-track approach to relieving this problem would be for the FCC to authorize DTV booster deployments by each part 73 licensee within its DTV station service area. The part 73 booster rules can and should be separate from the part 74 rules. A comprehensive interference analysis is performed as part of the existing process for each part 73 DTV station to obtain its main station license. It is a much simpler process to add low power boosters within an existing DTV service area in such a way as to provide improved

22

coverage while adding little additional field strength at the noise-limited contour. This type of deployment can bring coverage benefit with little risk of harmful interference to adjoining service areas.

The FCC has been conducting a biennial review of the new DTV service. The biennial review process may provide a convenient vehicle to incorporate suitable part 73 DTV booster rules.DTV broadcasters need the ability to deploy on-channel boosters to improve signal coverage in many areas. With careful analysis and planning, on-channel booster deployment is technically feasible to overcome terrain-shielded coverage gaps within a DTV service area. The FCC must be encouraged to adopt an expedited licensing procedure and early availability of appropriate regulations to help the DTV rollout reach more viewers than can be served by the primary DTV stations alone.

CHAPTER 3: RESEARCH METHODOLOGY

3.1   Introduction

From the phase 1 study, researcher can make a conclusion whether to choose a suitable hardware and software in this project. Many aspects had been taken to make this study going smoothly and researcher doesn't have to face much problem when this project is running. Researcher also had prepared the time length, so that this project can be doing according as a plan. Figure 3.1

The researcher will apply the parameter that has been chosen to adapt to the project development phase. The main point of a brief statement. The methodology comprises the following stages:-

- ➤ Planning phase
- ➤ Analysis phase
- ➤ Design phase

For the next phase the methodology uses comprises of these few next stages:

- ➤ Development phase
- ➤ Implementation phase
- ➤ Testing phase
- ➤ Conclusion and suggestion phase

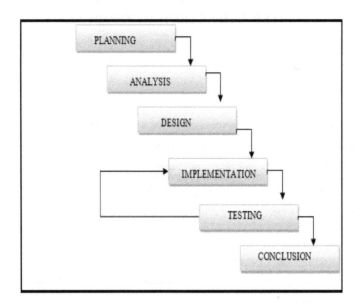

Figure 3.1: Waterfall Development System Analysis and Design

3.2 Design Method – Waterfall Based Methodology

Waterfall development is the original structured design methodology. In the methodology, overall project are break into a series of version that are developed sequentially. The advantage is quickly getting a useful project into that hand of user. A project also may require significant rework because will be made changes from time to time. When changes do occur, it means going back to the initial phases and following the changes through each of the subsequent phases in turn.

(Denis, Haley, Tegarden, 2005)

3.2.1   Planning Phase

Researcher had been given chance to select their preferred final year project title as on list, researcher had choose a title "**Wifi Signal Booster with Stir Frying Pan**".

In this first stage, the scope of the project is defined along with the approach to be taken to deliver the desired outputs. It is the phase within which the problem is identified, the solution ids agreed, a project formed to produce the solution.

3.2.1.1 Gathering Information

Lot of information had been doing by researcher either with supervisor or between team members. This is including internet, magazines, and books. For this method, researcher had done in doing research covered for wireless, wifi booster and product.

3.2.1.2 Seek Advice

Looks for professional for advice, where it can be done, researcher try get the information from lecturer, friends and also from the forum in the internet. Comment and idea from the judge also researcher take a referred to fix the problem.

3.2.1.3 Case Study

Definition case study taken from Wikipedia Free Encyclopedia, "Case study defined a phenomenon within its real-life context. Case study research mean

26

single and multiple case studies, can include quantitative evidence, relies in multiple sources of evidence and benefits from the prior development of theoretical proposition. "

3.2.2   Analysis Phase

The researcher has identified the signal strength on a typical antenna. The found out that the results of the signal vary depending on the location and the obstacle around it. The purpose to make sure requirement for the software or hardware will be captured and prioritized to be suitable to the scope and financial constraints of the project. In this first stage, the scope of the project is defined along with the approach to be taken to deliver the desired outputs. It is the phase within which the problem is identified, the solution ids agreed, a project formed to produce the solution.

The analysis phase involves creating a suite of planning documents to help guide the team throughout the project delivery. This first stage should include a detailed identification and assignment of each task until the end project. It should also include a risk analysis and a definition a criteria for the successful completion of each deliverable.

3.2.2.1 Project Plan

The creation of a comprehensive Project Plan is critical to the success of the project. It is indentifies the project phase and task to be undertaken to complete the project. It identifies the sequencing, duration and dependencies of task as well the generic resource and financial expenditures required to complete the project. The design Wifi Booster with Frying Pan is shown figure 3.2:

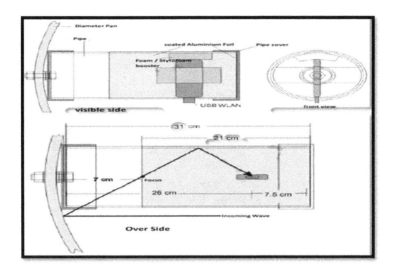

Figure 3.2: Propose Wifi Booster design

3.2.2.2 Resources Plan

The detailed assessment of the required to undertake the project should be made during this phase. Te required as network equipment, network material and labor are identified. Timeline and costing also is identifies during this phase.

3.2.3 Design Phase

This stage involves the execution of each activity and task listed in the project plan. While the wifi booster with frying Pan in process, a series of management process are undertaken to monitor and analyzed the output by the project. Then decides how the project will operate in terms of software, and hardware. Below is the list that will be used during the designing process.

28

3.2.3.1 Resources

(i) Hardware

Hardware that used for these projects are:

1. Pan
2. USB Wireless LAN Merk SMCWUSB-G 802.11g Wireless USB.
3. Pvc Pipe.
4. Pvc Pipe cover
5. Aluminium Foil
6. Foam / Styrofoam
7. USB Extension Cable
8. Hacksaw
9. Nut & bolt
10. Double tape.
11. Ballpoint / Markers
12. Wireless Access Point
13. U Bolts

(ii) Software

Software that used for these projects are:

1. Microsoft Word
2. Microsoft Project
3. Netstumbler
4. Access Point
5. USB Wifi
6. Backtrack

3.2.4   Implementation Phase

The solution is implemented to solve the problem specified in the project's requirements. Implementation is a hardware and software setup phase. Researchers provide tools are used to setup wifi booster. Apply wifi booster with frying pan into Access Point and configure using Backtrack hacking to find the nearest wireless signal and its signal strength.

3.2.5   Testing Phase

As the execution progresses, groups across the organization become more involved in planning for final testing, troubleshoot, and support. Testing using Backtrack to hacking wifi network forget the WEP key and will see that a key appear in front and we use to wifi higher signal

3.2.5.1 Testing Antenna

1. Install drivers
2. USB Wifi is not plugged into a USB port Notebook / PC
3. Insert the driver CD and follow the steps to complete installation
4. Wifi Connect the USB cable into a USB port Notebook via USB cable
5. If USB Wifi is detected means that the installation was successful

3.2.6   Conclusion Phase

For this phase is involved of final result to the client. This project covered a series of activities that includes:

   i.   Assessing whether the objective of the project have been met.

  ii.   Identifying the outstanding items (activities and task)

 iii.   Listing the activities that required handing over documentation.

Final activity can be review as an overall by how well it performed against the objective in the planning phase.

3.3   Project Requirement

3.3.1   Hardware

Hardware is the main, to the success of WiFi Booster project with the frying pan. Here describe this stage for some commonly built Wifi Booster. Pan figure 3.3, USB Wireless LAN Merk SMCWUSB-G 802.11g Wireless USB figure 3.4, Pvc figure 3.5.

Figure 3.3: Pan

Figure 3.4: USB Wireless LAN Merk SMCWUSB-G 802.11g Wireless USB

Figure 3.5: PVC pipe

3.3.2 Software

Panbolic antenna consists of 3 main parts:

1. Parabolic-shaped reflector using the Frying Pan

2. Sensitive parts tube-shaped antenna contains a USB WLAN

3. Cable connecting the antenna to the computer

Testing antenna:

1. Install drivers

2. USB Wifi is not plugged into a USB port Notebook / PC

3. Insert the driver CD and follow the steps to complete installation

4. Wifi Connect the USB cable into a USB port Notebook via USB cable

5. If USB Wifi is detected means that the installation was successful

Test the connection to the Remote Ap:

1. Do a scan AP

2. Trying connected to AP successful scan

3. Observing Signal Strength and Link Quality

4. Set IP USB Wifi accordance with its IP AP

5. Trying to test ping AP

6. Observing the ping test results

Measuring signal strength using Netstumbler (Optional):

1. Activate the program Netstumbler

2. Select the AP that in-detect

3. Observe the signal level (DBm) on the display Netstumbler

4. Repeat the steps above using a USB Wifi is not installed on antenna
FryPan bolic

5. Compare results

The working principle FryPan likes a satellite dish antenna, namely, placing the sensitive parabolic antenna at the focal point (pan) so that all electromagnetic waves on the pan will be collected and received by those sensitive parts. Here we discuss one by one.

Antenna FryPan bolic:

Why called the Frying Pan Bolic?

Frying Pan: pans, kitchen tools make cooking

Bolic: parabolic

FryPan bolic: parabolic antenna which is made fro m the pan

3.4   Budget and Costing

Description	Quantity	Estimation Cost
<u>Hardware</u>		
Pc/Netbook	3	RM1800*3
USB Wireless LAN Merk SMCWUSB-G 802.11g Wireless USB	1	RM180
PVC Pipe	1 (11mm long Approximately 32mm)	RM10
PVC Pipe cover	2 (11mm)	RM10
Pan	1 (36mm)	RM30
Aluminum Foil	1	RM8
Foam / Styrofoam	1	RM5
USB Extension Cable	1	RM20
Nut & bolt	10 (4mm)	RM5
TOTAL		**RM2068**

Table 1: Cost and Budget hardware

Description	Quantity	Estimation Cost
SOFTWARE		
Window XP	1	RM300
Backtrack 4	1	RM0
Microsoft Project	1	RM0
Microsoft Office	1	RM0

Table 2: Cost and Budget software

3.5   Project Timeline

Project time line is plan by using Microsoft Project to create the structure dateline diagram. The duration for this project is one year. Every phase has been identified and planned systematically to ensure the project will meet the dateline.

This project has consisted one phases:

i   Phase 1 which included Planning, Analysis and Design had been done in early June until October. Then Implementation, Testing and Conclusion had done until end of April 2011. (Refer to appendix to see the Gantt chart)

CHAPTER 4: PRODUCT DEVELOPTMENT

4.1   Product Development

Figure 4.1: Frying Pan Antenna

Figure 4.2: Cookware Antenna

Figure 4.3: Horn Antenna

4.1.1 Collect the part (First Stage)

The Researcher needs:

- USB RJ45 extension Adapter.
- Nuts and bolts size 13cm for antennas.
- The cover of the Pvc Pipe 4 "1 pair
- Frying Pan, cookware and cardboard
- Wireless USB Dongle
- Driller
- Aluminum foil

4.1.1.1 The Connector

USB RJ45 extension Adapter connector allows to connect wireless USB Dongle device to we are laptop. These can be found at electronics stores internet suppliers.

4.1.1.2 Nuts and Bolts

The reseacher needs the nuts and bolts for to go through the connector and the frying pan, Chinese cookware and Horn antenna.

4.1.1.3 Antennas

Frying Pan (Figure 4.1) with a diameter of at least 36mm, a Cookware (Figure 4.2) with a diameter of at least 28mm and a Horn antenna (Figure4.3) with a length 30mm, height and width 26mm.

4.1.1.4 USB Dongle

We use MERK SMCWUSB-G 802.11g Wireless USB Dongle for our project and PVC Pipe 11mm long approximately 32mm

4.1.1.5 Aluminum Foil

The reseacher use aluminum foil for wrapper to the PVC pipe and the cover of the PVC pipe to trap signal

4.1.2 Tools need

- Drilling machine
- Heavy duty cutter knife
- Ruler
- Notebook / PC

4.1.3 Panbolic antenna consists of 3 main parts

- Parabolic-shaped reflector using the Frying Pan, Chinese cookware and horn antenna
- Horn antenna made cardboard and aluminum fail
- A circular waveguide attached to both reflectors
- Cable connecting the antenna to the computer

4.1.4 Measuring signal strength using Backtrack

- Booting Backtrack
- Creating the partitions
- Creating the file systems
- Mount the devices
- Backtrack installer
- Installation is over, reboot Backtrack

4.1.5 Measuring signal strength using Netstumbler (Optional):

- From the Start Menu, the NetStumbler application link is clicked
- Once activated, one available AP from the list is selected
- The signal level from the selected AP is observed and recorded
- The steps above are repeated for the case where the WLAN USB dongle is not attached to any antenna
- Result for different cases are compared

The working principle Frying Pan likes a satellite dish antenna, namely, placing the sensitive parabolic antenna at the focal point (pan) so that all electromagnetic waves on the pan will be collected and received by the circular waveguide. Here we discuss one by one.

4.1.6 Some of the advantages antenna PanBolic:

- To increase the range of wireless LAN is required an external antenna with a gain higher than the standard antenna.
- No modification work on the RF system so no need to worry with SWR problem
- No need external power supply, because the power supply is taken from Wi-Fi USB port of Desktop or notebook PC, making it easier when outdoor live test using notebook
- Controllable beam width
- Being large or small dependant on design
- High gain
- Very much configurable dependant on usage

4.1.7 Pan shaped parabolic reflector using

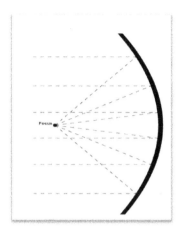

Figure 4.4: Feed Focus parabolic reflector antenna showing design

For this project, a frying pan (D=36 cm) and a cookware (D=28 cm) are used. In term of size, bigger diameter gives better reception of electromagnetic waves. The most important thing is the determination of the focal point for the frying pan. In order to that, we can use the following figure 4.5:

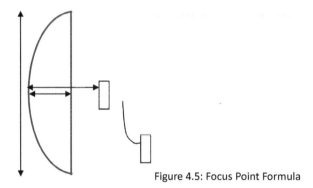

Figure 4.5: Focus Point Formula

4.1.7.1.1   Frying pan and cookware results

D (m)	d (m)	f (m)	G (dB)
0.28	0.09	0.054	13.94
28	9	5.44	<=== in cm

Table 3: Focus point for cookware antenna result

D (m)	d (m)	f (m)	G (dB)
0.36	0.1	0.081	16.12
36	10	8.1	<=== in cm

Table 4: Focus point for frying pan antenna result

4.1.8   Circular waveguide design

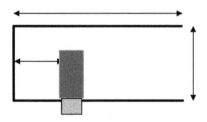

Figure 4.6: Circular waveguide antenna showing design values

Instructions the formula **Circular waveguide:**

$$Lg = \frac{L}{\sqrt{1 - (L/Lo)^2}}$$

L = (3*10 ^ 8/(frequency(f) * 10 ^ 9))*1000

Lo = 3.4 * Diameter (D)/2

Lg = L/($\sqrt{1- (L/Lo)^2}$))

4.1.8.1 Circular waveguide antennas results

Freq. Wifi	f	2.437	GHz
	L	123.102	mm
Feeder Diameter	D	110	mm
	Lo	187	mm
	(L/Lo)^2	0.43336	
	1 - (L/Lo)^2	0.56664	
	$\sqrt{1 - (L/Lo)^2}$	0.75276	
	Lg	163.535	mm
Position RF feed	**Lg/4**	**40.8839**	mm
Feeder Length	3/4 Lg	122.652	mm

Table 5: Calculation circular waveguide for pan and cookware antennas

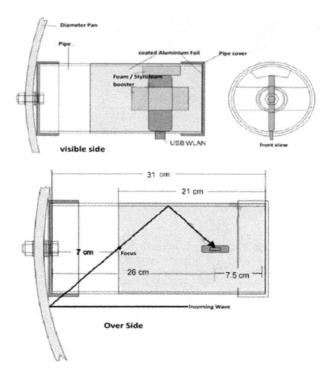

Figure 4.7: Design Visible and Over side design

4.1.9 Construction of the pan-shaped parabolic reflector antenna

1. A PVC pipe with the length of 31 cm is prepared. Then, the feeder size of the pipe is determined using the following

    i.   (F)=D/2(16*d) = feeder area

For our case:

    a) The diameter of the dish,D=14cm

    b) The Length of the visible side, d=7cm

Figure 4.8: Patch the aluminum foil

The inside of the PVC cover and the feeder area of the PVC pipe were patched with aluminum.

2. Make a hole on the frying pan and the PVC cover with using drill.

Figure 4.9: Punch 1 holes on the pan

3. Make hole on the lid of the PVC with the range same on the USB Wireless LAN Merk SMCWUSB-G 802.11g Wireless USB. Can be seen in Figure 4.10 and Figure 4.11:

Figure 4.10: Make hole on the lid of the PVC

Figure 4.11: Make hole on the lid of the PVC

4. Install the lid of the PVC with the pan.
5. Connect the USB WLAN on the Tube and to strengthen its position flops with Foam / Styrofoam and from USB WLAN has entered into a PVC pipe. Here we are using Cat6 or 1-port USB Superbooster Dongle - receiver cable to be connected to USB WLAN.

4.1.10 Boost Wifi Signal

1. Positioning is very important
   - To place the router or wifi booster in an open position such as corridor or brick walls.
2. Add an additional wireless access point repeater
   - They can be configures as gateways, client, repeater and bridges and to extend the distance of the signal.
3. Change the wifi channel
   - Operates in the 2.4 GHz frequency band and speed of up to 54Mbps. Changing the channel would reduce some interference.

4.1.11 Sensitive Antenna Tube

The tube shape so sensitive can be seen in figure 4.11 (picture B), in the form of Pvc Pipe that was placed inside a USB WLAN (picture C). The tubes can be used PVC Pipe and 31 cm of length wrap with aluminum foil (Note! Pvc pipe 4" diameter 5cm), Close one end of pipe wrapped in Aluminum with Lid Pipe 4 ". The inside of the pvc Pipe lid must also coated Aluminum (picture D). Make a hole in the pipe to place the USB WLAN in the pipe.

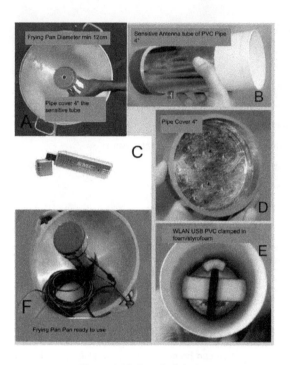

Figure 4.12: Detailed design

4.1.12 Horn waveguide design

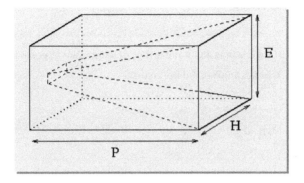

Figure 4.13: Horn antenna design

H = 0.26m (big side of the box)

E = 0.26m (small side of the box)

P = 0.30m (depth of the box)

Cutting two sides at once in a sheet:

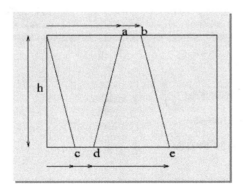

Figure 4.14: Cutting two side designs

CHAPTER 5: TESTING

5.1 Testing and result

This chapter will be explaining about the testing and the result after student doing the project. This includes testing method the analysis.

5.2 Testing Method

All the data were captured a strength signal so that student can analyze strength signal antennas performance on netstumler and wireless utilities. Three different kind of antennas used for testing; frying pan, horn and cookware. Due to limitation on hardware, the researcher has decided to test the three kind of antennas signal wifi booster on some of the wireless software in Kampung Baru and UniKL

5.2.1 Network Stumbler Analysis

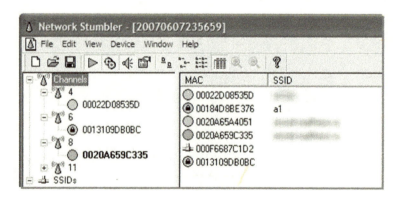

Figure 5.1: Netstumler interface

This for Windows only: Network manager NetStumbler lists all the wifi networks in we are area, their signal strength and whether or not they're passworded. Side by side the researcher also used the help of Wireless B+ Utilities, a great application for wi-fi.

The program is commonly used for:

- Wardriving
- Verifying network configurations
- Finding locations with poor coverage in one's WLAN
- Detecting causes of wireless interference
- Detecting unauthorized ("rogue") access points
- Aiming directional antennas for long-haul WLAN links

5.3   Results on Antennas

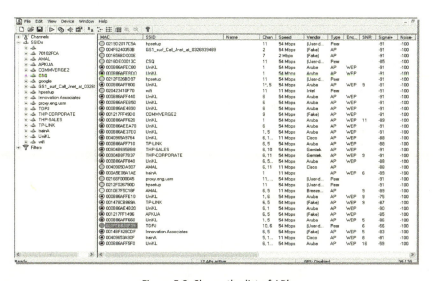

Figure 5.2: Shows the list of AP's

52

5.3.1 Results on Frying Pan Antenna

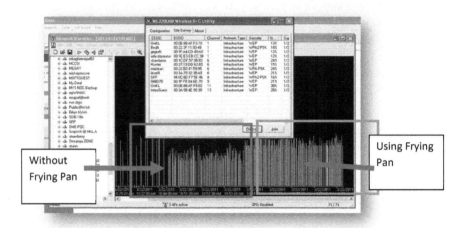

Figure 5.3: Shows with and without Frying Pan antenna results

Figure above show with and without frying pan antenna results. Students summarize that with frying pan antenna more than signal strength from without antenna. Before used frying pan antenna the signal is 19% and after to use 38%. In this part students concentrate at Ap's UniKl signal.

5.3.2 Results on Cookware Antenna

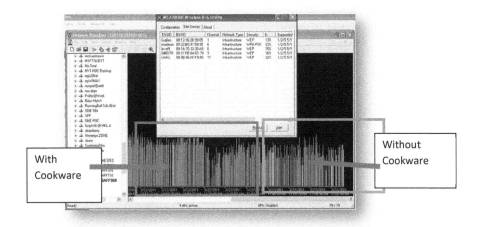

Figure 5.4: Shows with and without Cookware antenna results

Figure above show with and without cookware antenna results. Students summarize that with cookware antenna more than signal strength from without antenna.

5.3.3 Results on Horn Antenna

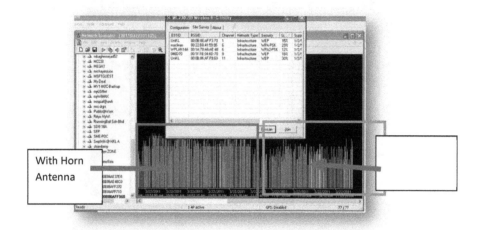

Figure 5.5: Shows with and without Horn antenna results

Figure above show with and without Horn antenna results. Students summarize that with horn antenna more than signal strength from without antenna. Before used horn antenna the signal is 19% and after to use 30%. In this part students concentrate at Ap's UniKl signal.

By using Network Stumbler, the researcher could actually get the MAC Address, SSID, Channel, Speed, and Vendor and determine whether it's an open network or an AP that is using a WEP key. Each AP's that is detected is categories by color.

     Green   : High Signal Strength

     Yellow : Medium Signal Strength

     Orange   : Low Signal Strength

     Grey   : No Signal

5.3.4   Comparison of three antennas signal to another place results

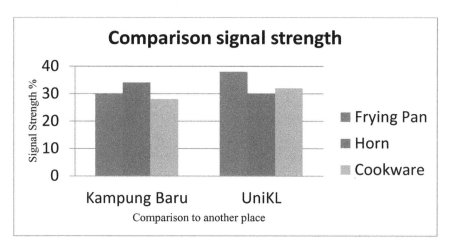

Figure 5.6: Comparison to another place results

Figure 5.6 shows the comparison strength signal to another place. If students at the Kampung Baru still have strength signal from Unikl. The higher strength wifi signal from Kampung Baru is horn antenna. Because that Horn antennas are very popular at UHF (300 MHz-3 GHz) and higher frequencies (we heard of horn antennas operating as high as 140 GHz). They often have a directional radiation pattern with a high gain, which can range up to 25 dB in some cases, with 10-20 dB being typical.

5.4   Results on Internet connection sharing

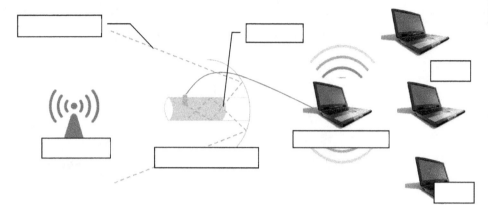

Figure 5.7: Reflector signal using Internet Connection Sharing

One computer, called the host computer or ICS terminal, which is connected to the Frying pan antenna and that has a separate connection to the other computers on network. We enable ICS on the Internet connection. The other computers on wifi network then connect to the host computer, and from there to the Internet through the host computer's shared wifi Internet connection.

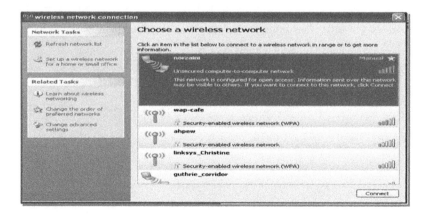

Figure 5.8: Internet Connection Sharing result

57

CHAPTER 6: CONCLUSION AND RECOMMENDATION

6.1   Conclusion

The primary objective of this analysis is to measure the performance use with and without antennas. Students collects the data from the analysis and comparison it to get results on netstumbler performance. From the analysis student found that if to use horn antenna, the higher have strength signal. Because of Horn antennas have a wide impedance bandwidth, implying that the input impedance is slowly varying over a wide frequency range (which also implies low values for S11 or VSWR). The bandwidth for practical horn antennas can be on the order of 20:1 (for instance, operating from 1 GHz-20 GHz), with a 10:1 bandwidth not being uncommon.

6.2   Recommendation

To enhance this Bolic Antennas Project some additional features can be added to it. In analysis, student recommends Rectangular waveguides, as opposed to circular and elliptical waveguides are by far the dominant configuration for the installed base of waveguides for compact systems like radar and inside equipment shelters. That is probably due to the generally greater rigidity of rectangular structures because the wall thickness can be easily made thicker than with circular. It is also easier to route and mount in close quarters, and attaching penetrating objects like probes and switches is much simpler (Refer to figure 6.1 and Figure 6.2).

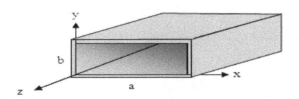

Figure 6.1: Rectangular waveguide design.

58

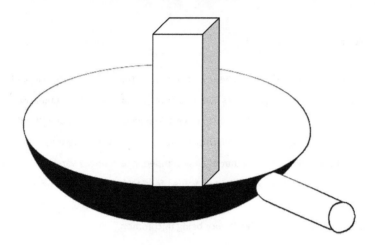

Figure 6.2: Shows the enhancement design to improve the Product.

He lowers cutoff frequency (or wavelength) for a particular mode in rectangular waveguide is determined by the following equations:

$$(f_c)_{mn} = \frac{1}{2\pi\sqrt{\mu\varepsilon}} \sqrt{\left(\frac{m\pi}{a}\right)^2 + \left(\frac{n\pi}{b}\right)^2} \quad \text{(Hz)} \qquad (\lambda_c)_{mn} = \frac{2}{\sqrt{\left(\frac{m}{a}\right)^2 + \left(\frac{n}{b}\right)^2}} \quad \text{(m)}$$

where

a= Inside width

b= Inside height

m= Number of ½-wavelength variations of fields in the "a" direction

n= Number of ½-wavelength variations of fields in the "b" direction

ε = Permittivity

μ = Permeability

www.ingramcontent.com/pod-product-compliance
Lightning Source LLC
Chambersburg PA
CBHW051213050326
40689CB00008B/1295